Eyes are everywhere.

But all eyes are not the same.

Bees have eyes.

EYES
ARE EVERYWHERE

Written by Polly Peterson
Illustrated by Yoshi Miyake

Cats have eyes.

Hawks and owls have eyes.

We have eyes, too.

Everywhere we look, we can see things

with our eyes.

We look at the flower.

We see this with our eyes.

Bees look at the flower.

They see this with their eyes.

We can see red and green

with our eyes.

Cats look at red and green.

They see this with their eyes.

We can see big trees with our eyes.

Hawks look at trees.

They see this with their eyes.

At night, we see in the dark

with our eyes.

Owls see in the dark.

They see this with their eyes.

Eyes can see.

Eyes can see everywhere.

But all eyes are not the same.